The Missions: California's Heritage

MISSION
SAN BUENAVENTURA

by

Mary Null Boulé

Merryant Publishers, Inc.
P.O. Box 1921
Vashon, WA 98070
206-463-3879
Fax 206-463-1604
http://www.merryantpublishers.com

Book Number Nine in a series of twenty-one

With special thanks to Msgr. Francis J. Weber, Archivist of the Los Angeles Catholic Diocese for his encouragement and expertise in developing this series.

This series is dedicated to my sister, Nancy Null Kenyon, whose editing skills and support were so freely given.

Library of Congress Catalog Number: 92-61897
ISBN: 978-1-877599-08-8

Father Junípero Serra

INTRODUCTION

Building of a mission church involved everyone in the mission community. Priests were engineers and architects; Native Americans did the construction. Mission Indian in front is pouring adobe mix into a brick form. Bricks were then dried in the sun.

FATHER SERRA AND THE MISSIONS: AN INTRODUCTION

The year was 1769. On the east coast of what would soon become the United States, the thirteen original colonies were making ready to break away from England. On the west coast of our continent, however, there could be found only untamed land inhabited by Native Americans, or Indians. Although European explorers had sailed up and down the coast in their ships, no one but American Indians had explored the length of this land on foot . . . until now.

To this wild, beautiful country came a group of adventurous men from New Spain, as Mexico was then called. They were following the orders of their king, King Charles III of Spain.

One of the men was a Spanish missionary named Fray Junípero Serra. He had been given a tremendous job; especially since he was fifty-six years old, an old man in those days. King Charles III had ordered mission settlements to be built along the coast of Alta (Upper) California and it was Fr. Serra's task to carry out the king's wishes.

Father Serra had been born in the tiny village of Petra

on the island of Mallorca, Spain. He had done such an excellent job of teaching and working with the Indians in Mexican missions, the governor of New Spain had suggested to the king that Fr. Serra do the same with the Indians of Alta California. Hard-working Fray Serra was helped by Don Gaspár de Portolá, newly chosen governor of Alta California, and two other Franciscan priests who had grown up with Fr. Serra in Mallorca, Father Fermin Lasuén and Father Francisco Palóu.

There were several reasons why men had been told to build settlements along the coast of this unexplored country. First, missions would help keep the land as Spanish territory. Spain wanted to be sure the rest of the world knew it owned this rich land. Second, missions were to be built near harbors so towns would grow there. Ships from other countries could then stop to trade with the Spaniards, but these travelers could not try to claim the land for themselves. Third, missions were a good way to turn Indians into Christian, hard-working people.

It would be nice if we could write here that everything went well; that twenty-one missions immediately sprang up along the coast. Unfortunately, all did not go well. It would take fifty-four years to build all the California missions. During those fifty-four years many people died from Indian attacks, sickness, and starvation. Earthquakes and fires constantly ruined mission buildings, which then had to be built all over again. Fr. Serra calmly overcame each problem as it happened, as did those priests who followed him.

When a weary Fray Serra finally died in 1784, he had founded nine missions from San Diego to Monterey and had arranged the building of many more. Fr. Lasuén continued Fr. Serra's work, adding eight more missions to the California mission chain. The remaining four missions were founded in later years.

Originally, plans had been to place missions a hard day's walk from each other. Many of them were really quite far apart. Travelers truly struggled to go from one mission to another along the 650 miles of walking road known as El Camino Real, The Royal Highway. Today keen eyes will sometimes see tall, curved poles with bells hanging from them sitting by the side of streets and highways. These bell poles are marking a part of the old El Camino Real.

At first Spanish soldiers were put in charge of the towns which grew up near each mission. The priests were told to handle only the mission and its properties. It did not take long to realize the soldiers were not kind and gentle leaders. Many were uneducated and did not have the understanding they should have had in dealing with people. So the padres came to be in charge of not only the mission, but of the townspeople and even of the soldiers.

The first missions at San Diego and Monterey were built near the ocean where ships could bring them needed supplies. After early missions began to grow their own food and care for themselves, later mission compounds were built farther away from the coast. What one mission did well, such as leatherworking, candlemaking, or raising cattle, was shared with other missions. As a result, missions became somewhat specialized in certain products.

Although mission buildings looked different from mission to mission, most were built from one basic plan. Usually a compound was constructed as a large, four-sided building with an inner patio in the center. The outside of the quadrangle had only one or two doors, which were locked at night to protect the mission. A church usually sat at one corner of the quadrangle and was always the tallest and largest part of the mission compound.

Facing the inner patio were rooms for the two priests living there, workshops, a kitchen, storage rooms for grain and food, and the mission office. Rooms along the back of the quadrangle often served as home to the unmarried Indian women who worked in the kitchen. The rest of the Indians lived just outside the walls of the mission in their own village.

Beyond the mission wall and next to the church was a cemetery. Although the headstones are no longer seen today, you can almost feel the Native Americans who lived and died at the mission. Also outside the walls were larger workshops, a reservoir holding water used at the mission, and orchards containing fruit trees. Huge fields surrounded each mission where crops grew and livestock such as sheep, cattle, and horses grazed.

It took a great deal of time for some Indian tribes to understand the new way of life a mission offered, even though the

Native Americans always had food and shelter when they became mission Indians. Each morning all Indians were awakened at sunrise by a church bell calling them to church. Breakfast followed church . . . and then work. The women spun thread and made clothes, as well as cooked meals. Men and older boys worked in workshops or fields and constructed buildings. Meanwhile the Indian children went to school, where the padres taught them. After a noon meal there was a two hour rest before work began again. After dinner the Indians sang, played, or danced. This way of life was an enormous change from the less organized Indian life before the missionaries arrived. Many tribes accepted the change, some had more trouble getting used to a regular schedule, some tribes never became a part of mission life.

Water was all-important to the missions. It was needed to irrigate crops and to provide for the mission people and animals. Priests designed and engineered magnificent irrigation systems at most of the missions. All building of aqueducts and reservoirs of these systems was done by the mission Indians.

With all the organized hard work, the missions did very well. They grew and became strong. Excellent vineyards gave wine for the priests to use and to sell. Mission fields produced large grain crops of wheat and corn, and vast grazing land developed huge herds of cattle and sheep. Mission life was successful for over fifty years.

When Mexico broke away from Spain, it found it did not have enough money to support the California missions, as Spain had been doing. So in 1834, Mexico enforced the secularization law which their government had decreed several years earlier. This law stated missions were to be taken away from the missionaries and given to the Indians. The law said that if an Indian did not want the land or buildings, the property was to be sold to anyone who wished to buy it.

It is true the missions had become quite large and powerful. And as shocked as the padres were to learn of the secularization law, they also knew the missions had originally been planned as temporary, or short term projects. The priests had been sure their Indians would be well-trained enough to run the missions by themselves when the time came to move to other unsettled lands. In fact, however, even after fifty years the California Indians were still not ready to handle the huge missions.

Since the Indians did not wish to continue the missions, the buildings and land were sold, the Indians not even waiting for money or, in some cases, receiving money for the sale.

Sad times lay ahead. Many Indians went back to the old way of life. Some Indians stayed on as servants to the new owners and often these owners were not good to them. Mission buildings were used for everything from stores and saloons to animal barns. In one mission the church became a barracks for the army. A balcony was built for soldiers with their horses stabled in the altar area. Rats ate the stored grain and beautiful church robes. Furniture and objects left by the padres were stolen. People even stole the mission building roof tiles, which then caused the adobe brick walls to melt from rain. Earthquakes finished off many buildings.

Shortly after California became a part of the United States in the mid-1850s, our government returned all mission buildings to the Catholic Church. By this time most of them were in terrible condition. Since the priests needed only the church itself and a few rooms to live in, the other rooms of the mission were rented to anyone who needed them. Strange uses were found in some cases. In the San Fernando Mission, for example, there was once a pig farm in the patio area.

Tourists finally began to notice the mission ruins in the early 1900s. Groups of interested people got together to see if the missions could be restored. Some missions had been "modernized" by this time, unfortunately, but within the last thirty years historians have found enough pictures, drawings, and written descriptions to rebuild or restore most of the missions to their original appearances.

The restoration of all twenty-one missions is a splendid way to preserve our California heritage. It is the hope of many Californians that this dream of restoration can become a reality in the near future.

MISSION SAN BUENAVENTURA

I. THE MISSION TODAY

Some cities realize the treasure that is a mission in their towns. It would seem that Ventura, where Mission San Buenaventura is located, is such a town. San Buenaventura is right on the main street (the name of the street is really Main Street) of Ventura. The city has surrounded the mission with a plaza of fountains, and huge green lawns. Tasteful walls are placed around archeological digs with openings so you can look at what is being uncovered. All of this has been done with an effort at keeping the Mexican style of the mission blending with the town itself. There are no buildings blocking the church's view of the ocean, just as in mission days. It is a delightful setting, even though the mission finds itself in the center of a modern city.

The church is large and made of adobe and stone, with walls six and a half feet thick. The outside walls have been painted a light cream color with deep red trim outlining the eaves and part of the bell tower. The double front doors of the church are wood and have designs cut vertically into them to represent waves of water. These "River of Life" designs are found at many California missions. The roof is tile, replaced in 1976.

On the east wall of the church, leading from the garden to the church interior, is a very unusual doorway built in Moorish style. The archway of the door has been formed to represent two rivers, Ventura and Santa Clara, that flow near the mission. The center point of the doorway is where the rivers symbolically meet. Above the doorway is a design representing the mountains behind the mission.

Inside the church is the campanario, or bell tower. In it are five bells; one made in Paris, France, in 1956 hangs on the top level. Four old bells hang at the lower level. Two of the bells have the year 1781 on them, and one bell is marked 1825.

Inside the church one finds a genuine feeling of old mission days. Original handcut beams hold up the roof. From the ceiling are hung wooden chandeliers, work of the famous restorer of missions, Sir Harry Downie. The new chandeliers were made by Mr. Downie to replace those ruined when they were wired for electricity long ago. These new chandeliers are much more in keeping with the mission than the ones they replaced. Mr. Downie, a true artisan, also made the front and side doors of the church, fashioning them exactly like the originals.

To the left of the entrance is the small Father Serra Chapel used as a baptistry. A hand-hammered copper bowl from mission days serves as the font. On the main walls of the church hang fourteen Stations of the Cross paintings dating from 1809. Two side altars, one containing a four-hundred year old statue of Christ on the cross, and the other dedicated to the Blessed Mother, are close to the front of the church.

The main altar and reredos came from Mexico when the church was dedicated in 1809. Typical of the style of those times, the reredos is of wood and has four wood columns painted to look like marble. In the large center niche of the reredos is a statue of Saint Bonaventure, the patron saint of the mission. On the floor is the original tile laid by mission Indians. Three mission priests are buried beneath the tile by the main altar.

East of the church is a peaceful, well-tended mission garden. In the center of the garden is a modern fountain of blue mosaic tile. This fountain, built in 1976, is Mexican in style, but looks nothing like the original fountain of mission days. The original was built by mission Indians, decorated with a sculptured bear's head. In one corner of the garden sits the mission's old olive press. Two giant, stately eighty-year-old star pine trees grow at the front of the garden. Legend has it that the trees were planted there by a sea captain during mission times. He hoped to use them as masts for his ship one day. Each year at Christmas time the trees are lighted to celebrate the holy season.

The present-day rectory runs across the back of the garden. On the east side of the garden is an excellent museum. The original church doors are kept there, as are two wooden bells used at the mission in early days. Mission San Buenaventura is the only mission known to have used wooden bells. The museum also has a fine display of Chumash Indian baskets such as those being made by Indians at the time of the mission's founding.

Credit must be given to San Buenaventura's priests during the last thirty years for the fine job they have done in restoring the church. Unlike many missions, which had to be built up from rubble, San Buenaventura had to have added decorations such as false ceilings torn down. We can be grateful for the priests' work, for once again Mission San Buenaventura is looking the way it should.

II. HISTORY OF THE MISSION

Mission San Buenaventura was the last mission an aging Father Serra founded. The date was Easter Sunday, March 31, 1782. Fray Serra's plan, from the first, had been to found this mission third after Mission San Diego and Mission San Carlos in Carmel. His reason was simple. The Buenaventura site was midway between his first two missions. However, life is not as simple as planned, sometimes. So it was that Mission San Buenaventura became the ninth, not the third mission in the California mission chain. Even the name was not a certainty. Different explorers and priests called it by several names, until it was finally named for Saint Bonaventure.

The Chumash Indians who lived in the area were intelligent and quite willing to work for small payments, such as beads or clothing. The first buildings went up rapidly. These Indians were known for their well-woven baskets that could actually hold water, and for their large, strong canoes built to be rowed long distances in the ocean. With such talents as these, the Chumash were excellent help in building several missions.

In 1794, ten years after the first church was built, it burned down. It took fifteen years for the Indians to build the new, large stone and adobe church that stands today. Huge hand-cut pine and oak ceiling beams came from a mountain range to the north and were dragged by oxen down the coast for the church building. Dedication of the completed church was held in 1809. Three years later a terrible earthquake in 1812 badly damaged it. The bell tower collapsed and mission buildings could not be lived in for a while. Mission people moved to the hills for three months until it was felt safe for

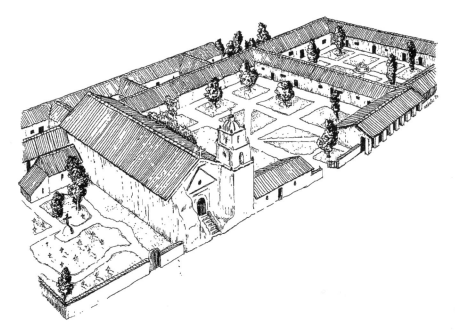

Original quadrangle of mission as it looked during mission days.

them to return. This was the only time in the history of the mission when it was without people. More than a year was spent repairing and reinforcing the church and mission grounds.

By 1816 the mission had reached its highest peak of activity, with 1,328 Indians living in the mission compound. A well-engineered irrigation system was worked out by the priests to bring water to the mission's dry farmlands. Part of the system included a seven-mile-long aqueduct carrying water from the mountains to a reservoir on a hill behind the mission. Today, if one searches, parts of the old aqueduct can still be seen.

Results of the fine irrigation system made the mission famous for its exotic fruits, herbs, vegetables. The British explorer, Capt. Vancouver told many people about the amazing products of the mission. He is known to have once carried twenty mule loads of fresh vegetables from the mission to his ship as he left.

During mission years there was a complete quadrangle to the east of the church. The church sat on the southwest corner of the compound and a cemetery was on the west side of the church. A grade school now stands where the old mission cemetery was.

San Buenaventura Mission was not as successful after the early 1820s. It had survived Indian attacks, pirate attacks, earthquakes, and fires, but when secularization came in 1834, the mission finally failed. In 1845 the mission had supposedly been rented for the next nine years. But Mexican governor, Pio Pico, sold the land illegally a year later and kept the money for himself. Then in 1857, an earthquake destroyed the original tile roof of the church and crumbled some of the rotting mission buildings. President Abraham Lincoln returned what was left of the mission to the Catholic Church in 1862.

Worse than all the disasters of nature that came to Mission San Buenaventura was the "disaster" caused by a well-meaning priest, Fr. Cyprian Rubio, in 1893. He modernized the interior of the church! When he was finished almost nothing remained of the old mission period church. Besides covering the ceiling and floor with wood panelling, he tore out the lovely hand-carved pulpit hanging on the side wall.

15

Only pieces of the pulpit have been found, but these were used in making a new pulpit, built in 1976. Fr. Rubio tore out the small, high windows along the side walls of the church and replaced them with tall stained-glass windows. Thanks to history-minded priests, the stained glass was removed in 1957 and the original style windows are once again in place. With the false ceiling and floor also removed, San Buenaventura can now proudly show its true heritage.

Restored sanctuary and side altars of mission church.

View from patio of Moorish-style side entrance to church. Door is carved with the common "river of life" design. Fountain in foreground is recently built and not modeled after original fountain.

OUTLINE OF
MISSION SAN BUENAVENTURA

I. **The mission today**
- A. Location
  - 1. Center of city of Ventura
  - 2. Plaza
  - 3. Archeological diggings
- B. Church exterior
  - 1. Walls
  - 2. Doors
    - a. Front doors
    - b. Side door
  - 3. Bell tower
    - a. Five bells
- C. Church interior
  - 1. Chandeliers
    - a. Sir Harry Downie
  - 2. Serra Chapel
    - a. Baptismal area and font
  - 3. Stations of the Cross paintings
  - 4. Side altars
    - a. Crucifix statue
    - b. Dedication to Blessed Mary
  - 5. Reredos and main altar
    - a. Statue of St. Bonaventure
  - 6. Tile floor
    - a. Priests buried near main altar
- D. Mission garden
  - 1. Fountain
    - a. Original fountain by Indians
  - 2. Star pine trees
    - a. Christmas lighting
  - 3. Olive press
  - 4. Rectory
  - 5. Museum
    - a. Original doors
    - b. Wooden bells
    - c. Indian baskets by Chumash
- E. Restoring of the church

Outline continued next page

II. History of the mission

A. Founded Easter Sunday, March 31, 1782
   1. Father Serra's last founding
   2. Named for St. Bonaventura
B. Chumash Indians
   1. Basket weaving
   2. Canoe building
C. Churches of mission
   1. Fire destroys first one
   2. Today's church
      a. Fifteen years to build; completed 1809
      b. Ceiling beams from nearby mountains
      c. 1812 earthquake damage
D. Mission life
   1. 1816 best year; 1,328 Indians
   2. Irrigation system
   3. Producing of fine fruits and vegetables
      a. Capt. Vancouver's visit
   4. Complete quadrangle east of church
E. Decline of mission
   1. Less productive after 1820
   2. Secularization
   3. Mission leased (rented), then sold
      a. Governor Pio Pico
   4. 1857 earthquake
      a. Original tile roof of church collapses
F. "Disaster" of Father Rubio
   1. Modernizing of church interior
G. Restoration
   1. Within last thirty years
   2. Uncovering of ceiling and floors
   3. Stained glass windows removed

GLOSSARY

BUTTRESS: a large mass of stone or wood used to strengthen buildings

CAMPANARIO: a wall which holds bells

CLOISTER: an enclosed area; a word often used instead of convento

CONVENTO: mission building where priests lived

CORRIDOR: covered, outside hallway found at most missions

EL CAMINO REAL: highway between missions; also known as The King's Highway

FACADE: front wall of a building

FONT: large, often decorated bowl containing Holy Water for baptizing people

FOUNDATION: base of a building, part of which is below the ground

FRESCO: designs painted directly on walls or ceilings

LEGEND: a story coming from the past

PORTICO: porch or covered outside hallway

PRESERVE: to keep in good condition without change

PRESIDIO: a settlement of military men

QUADRANGLE: four-sided shape; the shape of most missions

RANCHOS:	large ranches often many miles from mission proper where crops were grown and animal herds grazed
REBUILD:	to build again; to repair a great deal of something
REPLICA:	a close copy of the original
REREDOS:	the wall behind the main altar inside the church
*RESTORATION:	to bring something back to its original condition (see * below)
SANCTUARY:	area inside, at the front of the church where the main altar is found
SECULARIZATION:	something not religious; a law in mission days taking the mission buildings away from the church and placing them under government rule
*ORIGINAL:	the first one; the first one built

BIBLIOGRAPHY

Bauer, Helen. *California Mission Days*. Sacramento, CA: California State Department of Education, 1957.

Goodman, Marian. *Missions of California*. Redwood City, CA: Redwood City Tribune, 1962.

Snider, Ann D., ed. *Mission San Buenaventura, The Mission by The Sea*. No publisher, no date.

Sunset Editors. *The California Missions*. Menlo Park, CA: Lane Publishing Company, 1979.

Weber, Msgr. Francis J. *A History of San Buenaventura Mission*. Hong Kong: Libra Press Limited, 1977.

Wright, Ralph B., ed. *California's Missions*. Arroyo Grande, CA 93420: Hubert A. Lowman, 1977.

For more information about this mission, write to:

Mission San Buenaventura
211 E. Main St.
Ventura, CA 93001

It is best to enclose a self-addressed, stamped envelope and a small amount of money to pay for brochures and pictures the mission might send you.

CREDITS

Cover art and Father Serra Illustration: Ellen Grim
Illustrations: Alfredo de Batuc
Ground Layout: Mary Boule'
Printing: Print NW, Tacoma, Washington